Practical to Manage Costly Employee Turnover

Margaret Jacoby, SPHR

Book 1 in the series:
Practical HR Tools for the Small-Business Owner and Accidental HR Manager

Practical Tools to Manage Costly Employee Turnover

Book 1 in the series:
Practical HR Tools for the Small-Business Owner and Accidental HR Manager

Copyright © 2013 by Margaret Jacoby, SPHR

All rights reserved. This book or any portion thereof may not be reproduced or used in any manner whatsoever without the express written permission of the publisher except for the use of brief quotations in a book review.

Printed in the United States of America

First printing, 2013

ISBN-13: 978-1492293323

ISBN-10: 1492293326

MJMS Publishing
Mesa, AZ
www.mjms.net

Table of Contents

Introduction

How to Use This Book

Section 1: The Basics of Employee Turnover

Section 2: Understanding How Human Motivation Affects Your Business

Section 3: Steps to Creating a High-Retention, Engaged Workforce

Section 1:
The Basics of Employee Turnover

What is turnover?	1
Why should I care about turnover?	2
Where do I find turnover information about my industry?	3
How do I calculate turnover in my business?	3
My turnover rate is higher than industry competitors. What does that mean?	4
How do I measure the cost of my turnover?	6
Sample: Turnover Calculator"	7
Sample: "Checklist to Assess Cost of Turnover"	8–9
I know the turnover rate for my business and also understand the cost. What more do I need to know?	10
Sample: "Turnover Spreadsheet"	11
I run a good business, but people still leave. I don't understand why. Help!	12

Section 2: Understanding How Human Motivation Affects Your Business

Why do employees quit?   15

What keeps employees happy and ensures they stick around?   16

What can I do to motivate employees?   17

Section 3: Steps to Creating a High-Retention, Engaged Workforce

Step 1: Your clarity of purpose --organizationally and individually   19

   Sample: "10 Questions Entrepreneurs Can Ask to Focus Their Vision"   22–23

Step 2: Be smart about recruiting and hiring practices   24

   Sample: "Hiring for Retention"   26–27

Step 3: Develop strong work relationships and communication from day one   28

   Sample: "New Employee Orientation Checklist"   29–30

   Sample: "Employee Survey"   32–34

   Sample: "Develop Strong Work Relationships and Communication from Day One"   35–38

Step 4: Realize that performance management is not an annual event   39

Step 5: Keep your eyes open and be proactive   41

Stay in constant communication with existing employees.   42

Moving Forward

Free online download code for all HR WebForms   43

About Margaret Jacoby, SPHR

Introduction

Why this book? Who should read this book? About 14 years ago when I started my Human Resources (HR) consulting practice, I found the large majority of my clients were small-business owners who were good at their core business but struggled with managing their employees. They focused on building the business and the best widget or service they could produce or provide for the marketplace.

As they became more successful and hired on more folks to help the company succeed, they became more frustrated with keeping up with changing rules and regulations around employee management.

I started my practice in California where the vast majority of my clients based there faced the complex spider web of California labor laws. They needed some help to figure out what they needed to know.

Sometimes they turned this task over to the "office manager," the payroll clerk or the bookkeeper–someone who was not trained in HR and really did not want to learn about this aspect of the business. They agreed to the new responsibilities either to stay employed or make more money. They became "Accidental HR Managers" and they, too, needed some help.

It makes sense for these Accidental HR Managers to manage well and learn all they can to effectively support the employees and business owner.

If this sounds at all familiar to you, this book series is for *you*. It explains how to manage Human Resources -- starting with this book covering key elements of employee turnover.

-- Margaret

How to Use This Book

Whether you're in business to make money, make a difference, or for any other reason, you know that business success doesn't happen alone. You need a team. Your team may take a variety of forms -- from a collection of part-time contract workers to help you with specific needs to in-house staff members hired to fill functional roles within your organization. Regardless of the team-building strategy you choose, you realize that growing a winning team is necessary to drive results and create long-term success in your business.

But, growing a winning team to support the growth of your small business isn't a simple task. In fact, it's an area where many small businesses struggle, especially if you're accustomed to wearing multiple hats like so many founders and owners, as well as managers and supervisors. It's tough to trade the "I'll just handle it myself" point of view for the new habit of empowering, challenging and motivating others to grow and support the success of your business.

That's why I wrote this book. After working alongside owners of small, but growing businesses for 14 years, I've seen their struggles when it comes to hiring and growing a team. I wrote this book as an at-your-fingertips resource guide to support you in motivating, developing and retaining your team. When you apply the management principles and tactics in this book you'll not only grow a winning team, but also position your small business for competitive advantage and future success.

This book is broken into three main topic areas:

- The Basics of Employee Turnover
- Understanding How Employee Motivation Affects Your Business
- Steps to Creating a High-Retention, Engaged Workforce

Each section poses questions you may have about the topic. This lets you choose how to use this book. For instance, you can read this book from start to finish to get the full picture, or choose to read select questions that resonate with a particular issue or concern you're facing right now. Either way, use the Table of Contents to quickly navigate to the answers you need.

Section 1:
The Basics of Employee Turnover

- What is turnover?
- Why should I care about turnover?
- Where do I find turnover information about my industry?
- How do I calculate turnover in my business?
- My turnover rate is higher than industry competitors. What does that mean?
- How do I measure the cost of my turnover?
- I know the turnover rate for my business and also understand the cost. What more do I need to know?
- I run a good business, but people still leave. I don't know, or understand, why. Help!

Section 2: Understanding How Human Motivation Affects Your Business

- Why do employees quit?
- What keeps employees happy and ensures they stick around?
- What can I do to motivate employees?

Section 3: Steps to Creating a High-Retention, Engaged Workforce

- Step 1: Clarity of purpose—organizationally and individually
- Step 2: Be smart about recruiting and hiring practices
- Step 3: Develop strong work relationships and communication from day one
- Step 4: Realize that performance management is not an annual event
- Step 5: Keep your eyes open and be proactive

Section 1: The Basics of Employee Turnover

What is turnover?

Turnover is the rate at which you gain and lose employees. In other words, it's a measurement of how long employees tend to stay, contrasted against the rate at which they leave -- voluntarily or involuntarily. Turnover is often measured for individual companies, but industry turnover ratios are also tracked by the Bureau of Labor Statistics (www.bls.gov/news.release/jolts.htm). For example, turnover rates in hospitality jobs tend to be higher compared to government positions.

This is useful information to small-business owners, since having high turnover relative to your industry competitors may indicate an internal issue you need to address. High turnover can harm your company's productivity especially when you consider the investment you make in recruiting, hiring and training employees. Shorter than average tenure could mean you're not getting the best return on your hiring investment, and that is costly to a growing small business.

Why should I care about turnover?

Employee turnover is costly. The Bureau of Labor Statistics estimates that in January 2012, the median length of time an employee worked for an employer was 4.6 years. The Society for Human Resource Management (SHRM) reports the cost to hire an employee is more than $7,000. If you lose three employees a year that's $21,000 taken from your bottom line.

Can you afford to throw away that kind of money? But the cost hemorrhage doesn't stop there. Additional tangible and intangible losses you must account for include:

Tangible

- Cost to process termination
- Pre-employment costs to hire replacement
- Vacancy costs for temp to cover open position

Intangible

- Declining productivity due to change in team dynamics
- Increased stress and tension to meet increased workloads due to vacancy
- Loss of vital "tribal knowledge"

These are all very real costs for small businesses, and in many cases you will see the negative impact of turnover on your business very quickly.

Where do I find turnover information about my industry?

The Bureau of Labor Statistics (www.bls.gov/) provides an annual report of turnover by industry and region of the United States. The industries reported by the BLS are fairly broad. You may find more detailed information about turnover through professional organizations and groups related to your industry. For example, retail and telemarketing positions tend to experience double-digit turnover rates, while other industries see much smaller, single-digit rates.

How do I calculate turnover in my business?

Calculating turnover in your business is a fairly straightforward process. The most common calculation involves figuring monthly turnover. In this case, all you need is this formula:

Monthly turnover rate = (# of separations in month / # of employees in month) X 100

When determining the number of employees, be sure to include all employees on your payroll -- don't forget any employees on temporary layoff, leave of absence, or furlough. Do not include temporary workers paid through an agency or independent contractors.

Depending on the nature of your business, it might be more useful to calculate quarterly or annual turnover, and also compare turnover metrics between involuntary and voluntary separation. Let's look at the difference between involuntary and voluntary separation:

- **Involuntary Separation**: This is what happens when the employer, not the employee, makes the decision to terminate the employment relationship. Being *laid off* is considered involuntary, so is termination for performance, absenteeism, insubordination, etc.
- **Voluntary Separation**: This is what happens when the employee leaves the position; quits, retires, resigns, abandons job, fails to return from approved leave of absence, etc.

So, look at turnover in these two categories. For example, if you had an average of 125 employees in 2012, a total of 10 involuntary terminations, and 5 voluntary separations in the year, your calculations would look like this:

Involuntary turnover: (10/125) X 100 = 8% for 2012

Voluntary turnover: (5/125) X 100 = 4% for 2012

Total turnover: (15/125) X 100 = 12% for 2012

My turnover rate is higher than industry competitors. What does that mean?

High turnover can point to a variety of internal issues including:

- **Poor job fit**: The employee is not a good skill fit for the position, or does not mesh well with your corporate culture.
- **Substandard equipment, tools and facilities**: If you don't equip your employees to succeed and meet goals, they'll leave out of frustration.

- **No opportunity for growth**: Many employees are more engaged when their work provides opportunities for personal and professional development. A lack of growth can lead employees elsewhere.
- **Under-appreciation**: Most every employee wants recognition for his or her contribution to your company's success. Failing to acknowledge work can quickly demotivate.
- **Poor management**: Few employees thrive under managers who are disorganized, absent, or lack strong communication skills. Be sure your management team is equipped and able to support your employees.
- **Low salary**: Although money isn't the only reason people stay in their jobs, it is an important factor, so be sure your compensation structure is fair and equitable.
- **No buy-in**: Buy-in occurs when employees experience a sense of ownership in their job and in the company. They believe that their ideas and opinions count.
- **Poor training**: Without proper training, employees can feel they are being set up for failure. They aren't clear about what they should be doing and what equals success in their daily performance.
- **Living in Crisis/Chaos**: When employees are always putting out fires and working in a chaotic environment they get burned out, stop being productive and thoughts of leaving become common and widespread.

- **Negative corporate culture**: In this type of culture employees do not feel comfortable, acknowledged, or supported. Another common issue is that the rites or policies routinely change, resulting in confusion or inefficiency. There is lots of negative employee chatter.

How do I measure the cost of my turnover?

In addition to knowing the turnover rate in your business, you also want to determine the average cost for losing an employee. Two basic calculations can provide valuable insight to help identify and reduce turnover in your business:

- **Quick 'n Dirty**: To calculate a general cost of turnover when an employee leaves your business, use the following "Turnover Calculator" worksheet sample. Its formula uses an industry average to calculate your potential losses.

- **Advanced**: Use the following "Checklist to Assess Cost of Turnover" worksheet sample to itemize, line-by-line, the costs unique to your business -- from cost to hire a replacement, to cost of lost productivity while a position remains vacant.

Download the following two HR WebForms from MJMS's "Managing Turnover" link at www.mjms.net/hr-webforms. Use "MJMSHARDCOPYFREE" for the free, case-sensitive download code.

TURNOVER CALCULATOR

Annual wage for the job or employee $_____

Plus Cost of benefits (30% of salary) $_____

Multiple by 25% (average estimate)   _____ X 25%

Cost of turnover per employee $_____

Multiply by number of employees who left   __X__

Cost of Turnover $_____

(This formula is based on the model proposed by Saratoga Institute and Kepner-Tregoe Inc.)

NOTE: turnover costs are more complex than this simple formula. True cost includes investment in the employee's development, value of the departing employee's knowledge and experience gained while in your employ, lost productivity of that vacant position and lost productivity of those who must find a replacement.

CHECKLIST TO ASSESS COST OF TURNOVER

When one of your key people leaves for another job, use this checklist to assess the cost. Use the blank lines to add items relevant to your particular business or industry. Then use the formula at the end to see the dollar cost.

ITEM	ESTIMATED COST
Print & Internet Ads	
Search Firm	
Interviewing Costs (travel, hotel, meals)	
Interviewing time spent by manager & team	
Work put on hold until replacement found & on board	
Overload on team, including overtime during recruitment and training period	
Orientation & training time for replacement	
Lost customers	
Lost contracts or business	
Lowered morale & productivity (time spent talking about it around water cooler)	
Sign-on bonus and other perks	
Moving allowance	

Loss of other employees	
TOTAL COST	

I know the turnover rate for my business and also understand the cost. What more do I need to know?

Generally speaking, turnover is bad for business. You've calculated the cost to replace a valuable employee who voluntarily leaves and know it's high. Conversely, the price to keep, coach and manage a difficult employee is equally as high and may eventually lead to a costly involuntarily termination. To reduce turnover, it's important to analyze your data and take necessary steps to improve employee motivation and engagement. Here are a few steps to get started:

- **Maintain a turnover file.** This may be an electronic file folder on your computer, or hard copies of documentation you keep. The goal is to monitor the comings and goings of your employees by tracking:
    - Length of employment
    - Position held
    - Reason for leaving

See the following "Turnover Spreadsheet" sample. Or, download this HR WebForms file from MJMS's "Managing Turnover" link at www.mjms.net/hr-webforms. Use "MJMSHARDCOPYFREE" as the free, case-sensitive download code.

Margaret Jacoby

SEPARATION DATE	HIRE DATE	LENGTH OF EMPLOYMENT	POSITION HELD	REASON FOR LEAVING	NOTES & COMMENTS

NOTE: Use this spread sheet to track turnover. Go back at least one year and insert data to identify any trends or patterns to address. Turn Over Rate = (#terminations/total # employees) x 100.

Practical Tools to Manage Costly Employee Turnover

- **Watch for trends.** As you gather information about attrition, you will likely notice a trend. For instance, are there certain positions in your business often left vacant? What is the potential reason for this? Do you notice employees stay for a certain period of time, and then leave? Are they moving to a competitor, seeking more opportunities or leaving for some other reason?
- **Resolve problems immediately.** Once you've identified attrition trends, take immediate action to fix the problem. If exit interviews reveal people leave due to inadequate pay, research compensation data to determine if your pay is in alignment with the demands of the position and the industry. If people leave to pursue better career opportunities, either make sure you're communicating the limitations of growth in certain positions during the hiring process, or look for ways to build in growth opportunities for valuable employees you want to keep.

I run a good business, but people still leave. I don't understand why. Help!

Turnover isn't always a direct reflection of the quality and value of you personally, your character, or your business. Sometimes external factors beyond your control affect turnover. Even still, understanding the external issues facing all employers, not just small-business owners, will help you prepare for the challenges and make internal changes that can minimize the impact on your business.

Here are a few key external issues all employers must learn to navigate:

- **Smaller pool of potential employees:** Despite the struggling economy, the labor force is shrinking, which means fewer people are willing to (or need to) work. That means you're fighting to employ and retain workers from a smaller pool of potentials. Even more challenging are indicators pointing to a more mature workforce. In 1980, the median age for U.S. workers was 34.6 years. Today that number has increased to 42.8 years. That translates into nearly a decade of additional work experience average workers are bringing to their jobs, which translates into increased demands for higher compensation commensurate with that experience. Can your small business offer the salary and benefits workers desire today?

- **Higher demands, fewer benefits.** In response to the sluggish economic situation, many businesses do more with less, and employees feel the pressure. Many employees complain about longer working hours on a reduced salary or benefit plan. Employees are increasingly burned out, exhausted and stressed. Not only does this affect their productivity at work, but it also presents potential health issues forcing many workers to leave just to stay alive. Realizing you're working under similar pressure to do more with less, what might you do to help your employees maintain their energy, motivation, and health, while meeting the demands of your business?

- **Generational shifts in the workforce:** The workplace hears plenty of buzz about Baby Boomers, GenX-ers and Millennials, each with differing values and needs. Baby Boomers (born 1946–1964) are characterized by their hard work ethic, commitment and career focus. GenX-ers (born 1965–1981) were raised just as technology began to burgeon, and are known for seeking challenging, creative and diverse work opportunities. And, finally, Millennials (born 1982–2000) tend to thrive in workplaces encouraging rewards, promotion and development. How are you managing and meeting the unique needs of the generations found in your workplace?

Section 2: Understanding How Human Motivation Affects Your Business

Why do employees quit?

A variety of factors lead employees to leave a position, ranging from work-life challenges to boredom. Generally, people leave for these reasons:

- **Fear:** This is a big one. There are many things for an employee to be fearful about when it comes to their career. In response to daily news reports about the tough economy, employees may fear losing their jobs. So at the first sign of potential issues in your business, they jump ship and head to another more "secure" company. They may also fear becoming stagnant in a position showing little room for advancement. There could be growing concern that they just don't fit into your organization; they feel like a square peg shoved into a round hole.

- **Low job satisfaction**: The absence of "salary" or "money" in this list may surprise you. But according to the *National Study of the Changing Workforce*, earnings and benefits account for just three percent on job satisfaction, while quality of work and co-workers tops the list at a whopping 70 percent! Yet, employers often place high value on compensation and benefits, and while those are often the attributes of a job that draw in new hires, it's not usually the primary concern when people decide to leave. Instead, employees find the greatest satisfaction in the work they do and the relationships they develop in the workplace.

- **Poor management**: Given the value employees place on workplace relationships, it makes sense that working for a good manager is essential to keeping top employees. Managers who constantly reorganize, change direction, show favoritism or create rigid internal processes and structures, risk losing the interest and engagement of employees. Eventually these types of management styles damage the morale and esteem of the staff, and, eventually, lead to a rise in turnover.

What keeps employees happy and ensures they stick around?

As with the reasons employees leave, there are equally as many reasons why an employee chooses to stay in a job. In many cases, money and the lure of a credible job title attract new hires into your company. But don't place too much value in those things for too long. It's what happens after the initial "honeymoon phase" of employment wears off that keeps employees happy and engaged over time.

The Gallup Organization spent years researching what engages employees, and discovered 12 statements -- the *Gallup Q12*®-- that best predict employee and workplace performance:

- I know what is expected of me at work.
- I have the materials and equipment I need to do my work right.
- At work, I have the opportunity to do what I do best every day.
- In the last seven days, I have received recognition or praise for doing good work.
- My supervisor, or someone at work, seems to care about me as a person.
- There is someone at work who encourages my development.
- At work, my opinions seem to count.
- The mission or purpose of my company makes me feel my job is important.
- My associates or fellow employees are committed to doing quality work.
- I have a best friend at work.
- In the last six months, someone at work has talked to me about my progress.
- This last year, I had opportunities at work to learn and grow.

When you closely examine each of the 12 questions, you'll notice a common theme -- meaning and relationships. At the end of the day, what people want most from their work is an opportunity to use their talents in a meaningful way alongside people they enjoy. If you can provide those things, you can grow a winning team.

What can I do to motivate employees?

While the promise of pay raises and promotions may initially woo an employee, those external drivers lose their effectiveness quickly. Rather, intrinsic motivation is key to an employee's performance and on-the-job fulfillment. Intrinsic motivation comes from within. It's a natural desire to want to do something because it's fun, feels good, or is the right thing to do. Tapping into an employee's intrinsic motivation isn't always easy, but you can do it by following these steps:

- **Stand in their shoes.** Try to see your business, the workplace and the job from the perspective and mindset of your employee. To gain further insight, you can conduct employee interviews and surveys, or speak with customers who interact with your employees.

- **Listen and respond.** Rather than be in a position of always telling employees what to do, how to do it and when to get it done, stop to listen. Respond appropriately, always keeping in mind the unique perspective, values, and principles they bring to the job.

- **Get real.** People often come to work wearing a façade of how they "should be" rather than how they truly are -- this fosters inauthenticity and distance. Be a transparent leader, revealing your "realness" and, thus, encouraging your employees to show up as well. You'll be surprised at how tapping into individual potential and personal fulfillment changes how people show up and perform at work -- wow!

Section 3:
Steps to Creating a High-Retention, Engaged Workforce

The previous two sections of this book provided foundational information you need to create a high-retention, engaged workforce. This final section explains the five-step process you need to activate what you've learned to build and develop a winning team for your small business.

Step 1: Your clarity of purpose -- organizationally and individually

Chances are, when you started your small business you had a vision, or picture of what you wanted to create. Whether you associated that vision with the products and services you wanted to deliver, the lifestyle you wanted to create for yourself and your family, or a combination of the two, you knew what you wanted. As your business grows, that clarity is often lost in the busyness of getting work done.

Lack of clarity and direction can kill a small business and it can wreak havoc on your team. You're familiar with the saying, "the blind leading the blind?" That's what happens when you don't know where your business is heading. You can't effectively direct and motivate a team if you don't where to point them.

If you don't already have a clear short-term and long-term vision for your business, be sure to establish one before you move forward in this book. It's that important.

For guidance in this area, strategic business coach Jackie Nagel suggests 10 questions to help business owners focus their vision:

- What do you care about most?
- What are you working on that is making a profound difference for you and others?
- What gifts and talents are you currently using? What gifts and talents are currently not being utilized that you would like to put into operation?
- What does creating your vision mean for you?
- Where would you like to be in 3 years? 5 years? 10 or 20 years?
- What would you achieve if you were ten times bolder?
- What do you want more (less) of?
- If you had only one year to live, how would you want to live it?
- What 'theme' consistently runs through your life?
- What do you want to leave for others?

With a clear focus and purpose for your business, you're prepared to assess your human resources needs. In growing small businesses, hiring employees is often a spontaneous reaction to increasing work demands, when it should be a strategic decision based on what human resources you need to grow your business. As a result of reactionary-based hiring, you likely have employees who don't truly understand their job function and purpose.

Here's how to fix it:

- Gather any existing job descriptions you have for your employees.
- Sit down with each employee, individually, to get a better sense of their understanding of their job.

Review the following "10 Questions Entrepreneurs Can Ask to Focus on Their Vision" article sample. See the original article at www.synnovatia.com/business-coaching-blog/bid/139226/10-Questions-Entrepreneurs-Can-Ask-to-Focus-Their-Vision.
Or, download this HR WebForms document from MJMS's "Managing Turnover" link at www.mjms.net/hr-webforms. Use "MJMSHARDCOPYFREE" as the free, case-sensitive download code.

SYNNOVATIA

10 Questions Entrepreneurs Can Ask to Focus Their Vision

FOCUS
FOCUS
FOCUS
FOCUS
FOCUS

While the mission of your business centers on what you are called to achieve, your vision is the result of all you desire to accomplish. It is your ideal—your future. The vision you create for your business is the sustaining force that stimulates innovation, communicates passion, and inspires the masses to action. It is the vacuum that pulls you, and others, forward.

During a recent conversation with one of my clients, I asked if they had a long-term vision. I wanted to understand where this energetic and optimistic entrepreneur was going with their business. To this straightforward inquiry, they enthusiastically responded, "No, but I do have a 3 year lease." Don't you love it?!

Any entrepreneur who has ever launched a business can relate to this pragmatic vision. If it's not a lease driving our future, it's reaching an age milestone, starting a family, retirement, purchasing a first home, or a loan coming due that marks the future of our business.

In our rush to launch, it's not uncommon to focus on the tactical aspects of growing and developing our business with hopes to return to crystallizing our vision when time allows. Somehow, that time doesn't seem to present itself—until we find ourselves traveling along a road we never intended.

Although a few previously undefined twists and turns can prove to be a good learning curve for your business, they can also cause us to lose valuable time and opportunities. Consider your responses to the following questions to shed some light on the vision of your business and get yourself on the best track for your future:

1. What do you care about most?
2. What are you working on that is making a profound difference for you and others?
3. What gifts and talents are you currently using? What gifts and talents are currently not being utilized that you would like to put into operation?
4. What does creating your vision mean for you?
5. Where would you like to be in 3 years? 5 years? 10 or 20 years?
6. What would you achieve if you were ten times bolder?

www.synnovatia.com • PO Box 5267, San Pedro, CA 90733 • 800.398.6428

SYNNOVATIA

7. What do you want more (less) of?
8. If you had only one year to live, how would you want to live it?
9. What "theme" consistently runs through your life?
10. What do you want to leave for others?

Remember: To live without a clear image of your own vision is to live someone else's vision.

Author: Jackie Nagel is the founder and president of Synnovatia®, a strategic business service firm that collaborates with entrepreneurs and business owners to realize accelerated business growth. Learn more about growing your business by visiting www.Synnovatia.com or calling 310.519.1947.

© Jackie Nagel, Inc. DBA Synnovatia®

- Compare your existing job descriptions with the responses from your employees to uncover any gaps.
- Review the needs of your business to determine what job responsibilities should be added or removed, and then create a new job description.
- Meet with employees again to reset expectations and agree on next steps in performance.

Step 2: Be smart about recruiting and hiring practices

The person who accepts a job with a small business is different than one who chooses to work for a major corporation with thousands of employees. With this in mind, it's important to hire people who not only have the skill and knowledge your business needs, but also have attributes that would work well within a small-business culture.

Here are some important considerations as you look to fill open positions in your business:

- **Look internally first.** If there is an existing employee who is performing well in your business, why not consider grooming that person for the open position? Internal hires are less expensive to recruit, but they also have a fundamental understanding of your business, which saves you time in on-boarding and new-hire training.

- **Consider not hiring.** Is it possible for your business to operate effectively without filling a vacancy? To determine this, you'll need to conduct a thorough assessment of your business processes and productivity. You may discover inefficiencies that, once corrected, eliminate the need for a new employee.
- **Respond, don't react.** As much as possible, it's important to make good hiring decisions. Poor choices can lead to a long list of problems that can cause your business to stumble. When you feel the pinch to hire, pause. Assess your long-term vision, review existing job functions and productivity, and then make a strategic choice. Identify what skills are needed for the position
- **Realize interviews aren't enough.** An interview isn't a strong assessment tool for hiring. It's important to look at the whole candidate, including: job competencies, behavioral responses, personal charisma, communication, background and reference checks. Collectively, these elements help you make an informed hiring decision.
- **Think beyond the hire.** Finding a good hire and receiving an acceptance to your job offer may feel like conquering Mount Olympus, but your hiring responsibility isn't over yet! You must devote as much time to the on-boarding process as you did to the hiring process. Get your new employees off to a great start! Review the following "Hiring for Retention" sample worksheet. Or, download the HR WebForms file from MJMS's "Managing Turnover" link at www.mjms.net/hr-webforms. Use "MJMSHARDCOPYFREE" as the free, case-sensitive download code.

HIRING FOR RETENTION

BEFORE THE FIRST DAY OF WORK:

- Appoint a person to call before the new hire starts work - welcome them!
- Have the new hire complete paperwork on intranet, or send forms in mail
- Send a form of greeting such as a card, welcome basket, or other gesture
- Have HR rep call and answer questions about benefits and such
- Be sure new hire knows where to park, has pass or key card or other necessary item to access parking

DURING THE NEW HIRE'S FIRST TWO DAYS AT WORK:

- Have key employees sit down with new person and discuss what it is like to work there - new employee gets support network and key employees build leadership skills
- Take digital photo of new hire and create a flyer to post detailing their background, hobbies, experiences
- Introduce new employee to CEO or owner
- Provide a "new employee" parking spot for first week
- Provide copy of company's mission and vision statement
- Be sure new employee has a phone and e-mail directory of everyone in company
- Assign an employee who enjoys working with people as a "buddy" to the new employee - "buddy" is responsible for helping new person settle in and get acquainted with the worksite
- Be sure the new employee's worksite is properly equipped - stocked with supplies, phone and computer are operable
- Have a company t-shirt or mug or other item for new person
- Have business cards already printed and ready
- Take the new person to lunch to meet the team
- Hang a welcome sign signed by the team members

- ◊ Put photo of new employee in local newspaper and company newsletter welcoming them to the organization
- ◊ Send the spouse or family some sort of welcoming gift
- ◊ Have a spouse's support group invite the new person's spouse to coffee
- ◊ Have a new employee lunch for spouses during the first month
- ◊ Minimize forms to sign and videos to view until a bit later in the week
- ◊ Take a team photograph

DURING THE NEW HIRE'S FIRST WEEK AT WORK:

- ◊ Have someone meet new employee after the first week and find out what went right and what went wrong
- ◊ Reward those employees who were helpful to the new person
- ◊ Put photos of the "go-to" people on a wall for the new person to see

Step 3: Develop strong work relationships and communication from day one

Traditionally, new employees undergo a New Hire Orientation process. For suggestions on what to include in yours, review the following "New Employee Orientation Checklist" sample. Or, download this HR WebForms file from MJMS's "Managing Turnover" link at www.mjms.net/hr-webforms. You may use "MJMSHARDCOPYFREE" as the free, case-sensitive download code.

Remember, new-hire orientation is more than a one-time, one-day event. Instead, it should be looked at as a process of integrating and acclimating a new employee to your company's unique culture and way of doing business. This process can take a few months, or may last a year or more, depending on your business.

Margaret Jacoby

NEW EMPLOYEE ORIENTATION CHECKLIST

Be sure the new employees have an opportunity to learn about every aspect of the organization. Look for ways to make the orientation comprehensive but not overwhelming.

Introduction to the Company
- History of the Organization
- Diversity policy
- EEO statement/policy
- Worksite Mission
- Employee Handbook
- W-4 and other payroll documents

Benefits, Compensation and Incentives
- Health, life, disability insurance
- Retirement benefits
- Pay procedures
- Performance evaluation
- Reward and recognition programs
- Ideas/suggestions programs
- Education assistance
- Career development opportunities
- Health and wellness opportunities
- Flextime policies

Leaves of Absence
- Return to work policy
- Maternity leave
- Leave without pay
- Sick leave/PTO
- Military leaves
- Jury duty
- Bereavement
- Family and Medical Leave Act (FMLA)

Work Environment
- Tour of worksite and important places, restrooms, coffee/break areas, cafeteria (if any), coat and personal property storage areas

- Parking for vehicles, public transportation routes
- Proper dress
- Standards of conduct
- Employee grievance procedures
- Smoking policy
- Safety and Security
- Computer system
- Equipment issue
- E-mail and use of Internet
- Phone system
- Copy machines

The best way to begin is to use the Gallup Q12® statements as a benchmark for new-hire activities. For example, question one says, "I know what is expected of me at work." When you consider that statement from a new employee's perspective, what might he or she need to make that a true statement? Here are a few ideas:

- An accurate job description
- An introduction to team and supervisor
- Performance plan with clear work expectations and goals

The second statement, "I have the materials and equipment I need to do my work right," might involve providing:

- A comfortable place to work (i.e. desk, chair, phone, laptop, etc.)
- Knowledge of where to find needed supplies or resources

As you move through Gallup's 12 statements, you'll begin to recognize what you need to incorporate in your on-boarding process to develop strong working relationships and communication practices with your employees.

Review the following two sample documents -- "Employee Survey" worksheet and "Step 3: Develop Strong Working Relationships and Communication from Day One." They can help you identify two or three specific to-do items associated with each of the Q12® items. Or, download these HR WebForms from MJMS's "Managing Turnover" link at www.mjms.net/hr-webforms. You may use "MJMSHARDCOPYFREE" as the free, case-sensitive download code.

EMPLOYEE SURVEY

In keeping with our goal to continuously improve, we want your feedback to measure our performance as your employer. We would appreciate your responses to the following questions. All responses will be kept strictly confidential and will be reviewed by _____. Only a summary of the responses will be shared with the management team.

NOTE: choices are limited to Strongly Agree; Agree; Disagree; Strongly Disagree (SA, A, D, SD)

STATEMENT	YOUR RESPONSE
1. I know what is expected of me at work.	
2. I have the equipment and materials to do my work right.	
3. At work, every day I have the opportunity to do what I do best.	

MJ Management Solutions, Inc.

www.mjms.net

PAGE 1

Margaret Jacoby

4. In the last 7 days, I have received recognition or praise for doing good work.	
5. My supervisor, or someone at work, seems to care about me as a person.	
6. There is someone at work who encourages my development.	
7. At work my opinions seem to count.	
8. The mission or purpose of my company makes me feel my job is important.	
9. My associates or fellow employees are committed to doing quality work.	

10. I have a best friend at work.	
11. In the last six (6) months someone at work has talked to me about my progress.	
12. In the last year, I have had opportunities at work to learn and grow.	

NOTE: Use this form to view the engagement of your employees. Then, use the Worksheet described in Step 3 – "Develop strong work relationships and communication from day one" to develop or revise New Hire Activities. For support in anayzing the results, contact us at 480-924-6101 or www.mjms.net.

MJ Management Solutions, Inc.

www.mjms.net

PAGE 3

STEP 3: "DEVELOP STRONG WORK RELATIONSHIPS AND COMMUNICATION FROM DAY ONE"

Below are the Statements based on the "Gallup Q12®" engagement survey. When you consider your employees' responses to each of the 12 questions, here are some ideas you might consider.

1. I know what is expected of me at work.
   - Develop an accurate job description
   - Facilitate introductions to team members and supervisors
   - Conduct a thorough new hire orientation and transition from applicant to employee

2. I have the equipment and materials to do my work right.
   - Provide a comfortable place to work (i.e. desk, chair, phone, lighting, etc)
   - Knowledge of where to find needed supplies and resources
   - Provide up-to-date, functioning equipment (computer, internet, tools, vehicles, etc.)

3. At work, every day I have the opportunity to do what I do best.
   - Provide meaningful work that uses the skills and talents of the employee
   - Encourage employees to use skills and abilities not related to job
   - Provide opportunities to assist in projects in other departments

The Q12 items are protected by copyright of The Gallup Organization, 1992-2004

4. In the last seven (7) days, I have received recognition or praise for doing good work.
   - Provide positive feedback on good performance
   - Award "spot" bonuses or rewards for "above the call of duty" performance
   - Award day off with pay after completion of difficult or long-term project

5. My supervisor, or someone at work, seems to care about me as a person.
   - Recognize special milestones in employee's life (birth of child, marriage, child's graduation from college, etc.)
   - Celebrate anniversaries of employment
   - Celebrate employee birthdays

6. There is someone at work who encourages my development.
   - Establish a performance plan with clear work expectations and goals
   - Provide training programs to enhance skills or develop new skills
   - Provide opportunities to rotate through different departments
   - Establish tuition reimbursement programs for employees attending college

7. At work my opinions seem to count.
   - Request employee feedback on projects or changes being considered
   - Request employee participation in selection of benefit programs
   - Encourage employees to make decisions without fear of retaliation

The Q12 items are protected by copyright of The Gallup Organization, 1992-2004

8. The mission or purpose of the Company makes me feel my job is important.
   Communicate a clear vision for the company with all employees
   Share the strategic direction of the company with all employees
   Demonstrate the value of each job to moving the company mission forward

9. My associates or fellow employees are committed to doing quality work.
   Employees recognize the value of each other and support one another
   Employees who are not engaged are not retained by the company
   Encourage senior employees to mentor new and less-experienced employees

10. I have a best friend at work.
    Conduct social activities to allow employees to "get to know" one another
    Assign employees from various departments to team projects to foster building relationships and trust

11. In the last six (6) months someone at work has talked to me about my progress.
    Provide performance feedback regularly, not waiting for the annual review process
    Provide on-the-spot counseling by supervisors to correct performance issues
    Hold informal supervisor/employee feedback sessions quarterly or monthly

The Q12 items are protected by copyright of The Gallup Organization, 1992-2004

12. In the last year, I have had opportunities at work to learn and grow.
    Provide rotations through departments or job-sharing opportunities
    Provide opportunities for promotions instead of always hiring from outside
    Provide training in new technologies or equipment

Engagement is not something that happens once a year. This worksheet and the survey it supports are found in the short ebook *Practical Tools to Manage Costly Employee Turnover*. The ebook is filled with explanations, advice, worksheets, handy calculators, and more. You'll discover a solid foundation of information to help you manage your organization's HR issues... without the learning curve. Download the ebook at http://www.mjms.net/book1

For more specific assistance in analyzing the survey results or implementing some of these suggestions, why not talk to us and find out how we can help? We know that deciding to use outside expertise isn't easy--we will be privileged to earn your trust. Visit our website at www.mjms.net or call us at 480-924-6101 or 310-798-4569.

The Q12 items are protected by copyright of The Gallup Organization, 1992-2004

Step 4: Realize that performance management is not an annual event

I know few people who look forward to performance review time. It's the annual corporate ritual that stresses managers out and puts employees on the defensive. But it doesn't have to be this way, and when done well, performance management is actually a valuable retention tool for small businesses.

First, let's define performance management. According to a briefing from the Society of Human Resources Management (SHRM), "Performance management drives employee behavior to align with organizational goals and objectives. This alignment happens because (1) job responsibilities and expectations are clear, resulting in increased individual and group productivity; and (2) better information is available to use for compensation and promotion decisions."

Performance management begins with clarity of purpose as described in the previous article, "10 Questions Entrepreneurs Can Ask to Focus on Their Vision" (www.synnovatia.com/business-coaching-blog/bid/139226/10-Questions-Entrepreneurs-Can-Ask-to-Focus-Their-Vision). You may alternatively download this HR WebForms document from MJMS's "Managing Turnover" link at www.mjms.net/hr-webforms. Use "MJMSHARDCOPYFREE" as the free, case-sensitive download code.

This document will help you with both organizational goals and employee goals. If you've completed that step -- congratulations! You're on your way, but don't stop there. That's where most employers get derailed. Performance management is the consistent practice of measuring and monitoring your employees' performance against your company's performance.

At face value, this may seem like a lot of work, but here are some quick steps to ease the pain:

- Develop performance assessment tools -- an employee version and a supervisor version. There are some out-of-the-box tools available, or you may want to create one from scratch that's personalized to the needs of your business. This performance appraisal packet toolkit at www.mjms.net/hr-webforms will get you started.

- Communicate performance expectations to employees and supervisors. If this is a totally new process for your business, it will be useful to hold an all-hands meeting to share your performance management process and expectations. Distribute the assessment tools so everyone is clear about how their performance will be measured. This is also a great time to connect with employees and gather input or feedback on the performance process.

- Allow employees to self-manage their performance. Employees are adults who can responsibly manage their career growth, so let them. After employees meet with their supervisors to establish baseline goals and expectations for the year, each employee should monitor and track his or her performance. Employees can create a folder (a real manila file, or an electronic one stored on a computer) to store achievements, results and other performance-related materials.

- Require supervisors to manage employee performance. Unfortunately, too many supervisors fail to track their team's performance throughout the year, which means at performance review time, they're left trying to recall a year's worth of achievements for one or more employees. That's a near-impossible task for even the best supervisor. Similar to employees, supervisors should keep file folders for each member of their team to track achievements, results and other performance-related materials.

- Encourage quarterly performance meetings. Every three months, employees should invite their supervisor for a brief meeting to evaluate progress toward performance goals and reset objectives, accordingly. When both parties bring their "performance folders" to the meeting, the process is as simple as comparing notes and agreeing on next steps. This regular process of checking in not only fosters strong two-way communications, but also ensures no surprises at the annual performance review meeting.

Step 5: Keep your eyes open and be proactive

Ultimately, the best way to build a winning team for your growing business is to be aware and responsive to the needs of your business and your employees.

- **Don't ignore the signs.** Employees express their dissatisfaction in a variety of ways, from arriving to work late to doing just enough work to get by. Be observant. Notice when performance, attitude or habits shift in your employees, and take immediate action. Don't wait for the problem to grow. Communicate. Address issues early.
- **Learn from past employees.** When one of your best employees decides to leave your business, find out why. The best way to do this is to conduct an exit interview, though you may discover more by interviewing the past employee's co-workers and direct supervisor.

Stay in constant communication with existing employees.

Periodically check in with employees to assess their satisfaction with work, salary and other important aspects of their job. Also, watch how they interact with others at work. Sometimes, simply seeing their faces light up in response to a specific event at work provides just what you need to uncover their motivation.

Any healthy, growing relationship is characterized by understanding and respecting one another's reasonable expectations, goals and boundaries, and that's exactly what you're fostering in your small business when following these guidelines and practices. As you take willing steps to develop and communicate clear purpose to your employees, you should find your working relationships improving, employee retention increasing, and word-of-mouth about your business being a great environment to work in spreading.

Moving Forward

Each section in this book posed questions you may have about this topic. Use the Table of Contents to quickly navigate to the answers you need.

Go back to the three topic sections as you consider the turnover in your organization:

- The Basics of Employee Turnover
- Understanding How Employee Motivation Affects Your Business
- Steps to Creating a High-Retention, Engaged Workforce

Read select questions that resonate with a particular issue or concern you're facing right now. Use the HR WebForms tools and worksheets in this book, all of which may be accessed online from MJMS's "Managing Turnover" link at www.mjms.net/hr-webforms. Use "MJMSHARDCOPYFREE" as your free, case-sensitive download code.

Even if Human Resources isn't your primary job focus and you think you need a little help, you can manage your HR duties professionally. If you got this far in the book, you have demonstrated you are serious about your responsibilities.

It makes sense for Accidental HR Managers like you to manage well and learn all you can to effectively support the employees and business owner.

This is the first book in the series *Practical HR Tools for the Small-Business Owner and Accidental HR Manager*. We invite you to identify your areas of greatest concern in the world of HR to add to the content of future books. Send an email book@accidentalhrmanager.com.

About Margaret Jacoby, SPHR

New author Margaret Jacoby compiles 30 years of diverse, real-life Human Resources and professional management experience into *Practical Tools to Manage Costly Employee Turnover*, book 1 in the *Practical HR Tools for the Small-Business Owner and Accidental HR Manager* series.

As owner of consulting practice MJ Management Solutions, Inc., for the last 14 years, she works closely with employees who take on a small-business organization's HR responsibilities without the benefit of formal HR training or background.

Margaret provides high-quality human resources services for these "accidental HR managers" in small and emerging businesses mostly in California, Arizona, and Hawaii. Margaret serves as an external consultant to a wide range of diverse organizations, from Native American communities in the Southwest to nonprofit service organizations nationwide.

She earned the nationally recognized certification of Senior Professional in Human Resources (SPHR) from the HR Certification Institute, Society for Human Resource Management (SHRM).

You can reach Margaret in Mesa, Arizona, at 480.924.6101, or in California at 310.798.4569. Learn more at Margaret@mjms.net or visit www.mjms.net.

Printed in Great Britain
by Amazon